Hard Curves

THE FANTASY ART OF JULIE BELL

Hard Curves

THE FANTASY ART OF JULIE BELL

TEXT BY NIGEL SUCKLING
FOREWORD BY HANK ROSE

Paper Tiger
An Imprint of Dragon's World
Dragon's World Ltd
Limpsfield
Surrey RH8 0DY
Great Britain

First Published by Dragon's World Ltd 1995

The catalogue record for this book is
available from the British Library
ISBN 1 85028 223 4 Limpback

Editor Fiona Courtenay-Thompson
Designer Nigel Coath at ProCreative
Art Director John Strange
Editorial Director Pippa Rubinstein

Printed in Singapore

*For Boris, without whom, in
every aspect of my life, I would
be in a different universe.*

Hard Curves

THE FANTASY ART OF JULIE BELL

Contents

Introduction

It's Tuesday afternoon. I'm in my office after a particularly frustrating morning. I need to hear a friendly voice, so I grab my phone, hit the appropriate speed dial number and wait. A soothing feminine voice answers with a sweet "hello" and I'm already feeling better. Julie Bell has a way of doing that. Now, please understand, I love talking with Boris Vallejo, her husband – who, as you probably know, is arguably the finest fantasy artist of all time. But soothing is Julie's job.

We all met several years ago, when my company started producing Boris' trading cards. My admiration for Julie was immediate. It is not often I meet a beautiful woman who can out-bench-press me, whip me at arm wrestling, and almost beat me in a foot race. These, though, are the talents hidden behind a soft-as-silk demeanour and an alluring charm. The talents she thankfully cannot hide are to be seen on the pages in this book, as well as on trading cards, calendars, book jackets, video games and many other products appearing throughout the world.

Without question, developing her talent in the same house as Boris has helped Julie to climb so quickly in the fantasy art field. Boris is a wonderful inspiration and teacher. He works with unflappable discipline and a dedication to his art that Julie has acquired not only by osmosis but also by hard work. In this book you will experience the Julie Bell style – a style far different from any other fantasy artist's way of expression.

The Julie Bell style is as complex as the artist herself. It reflects a life full of experiences, highs and lows, happy memories and, yes, many extremely difficult times.

Art is the extension of the individual. It is the purposeful exploits of one driven to create. The commitment to convey one's ideas to an art form is a deep human endeavour. It is the baring of the soul, a cleansing. Julie's art manifests her need to be recognized, accepted, talked about or respected. Art is the most graphic form of communication; the most time-consuming, most misinterpreted and often the most painful. It is work, and joy, and frustration, and sacrifice and love.

Hard Curves shows the range of a rising superstar. It also helps us understand what Julie is trying to tell us through her painting. In each piece there are so many turns, so many clues. The immediate response is one of emotion. We are absorbed into the painting by the action, which may be a fight-to-the-death battle or a seemingly innocent look of a beautiful woman. The range is unpredictable. Then the fun begins. The eye is trapped on metallic images that our mind tells us should not be there. The metallic skin has no restriction, no encumbrances.

It is as though this skin is not on the body. It is the body. It has no weight, only power. No negative aspects, only protection. Amazingly, this metallic veneer does not hide muscle, tendon and sinew, but accentuates the body's power and motion as though it possesses its own chrome consciousness. We see now Julie's total understanding of the human form, much of which was attained when she was a nationally ranked bodybuilder. She has a myriad of trophies and awards to prove it.

Beyond the metallic skin, or perhaps I should say beneath it, comes what is in my opinion the essence of Julie's gift. There exists in the interstices of Julie's paintings a sensitivity that is peculiarly hers. This sensitivity comes from an equation that combines one part mother, one part storyteller, one part bodybuilder. Add equal parts woman, protector, warrior and comedienne, and you may then begin to appreciate what Julie is communicating. Be the subjects of her art superheroes or villains, superhuman or mortal, you will experience an empathy for each being and discern its role in the piece.

Your first trip through *Hard Curves* will be a joyful, respectful ride through the world of fantasy. It will also be a catalyst forcing you to return again and again to these pages to re-enter Julie Bell's world of unforgettable images and feelings of metal and might, sensuality and sensitivity, and a special view of the world as communicated by a truly gifted young visionary.

After spending ten enjoyable minutes on the phone with Julie that Tuesday afternoon, swapping jokes and just rapping, I felt much better. My day certainly improved. Since you are probably not lucky enough to have her on your speed dial, I invite you to bring Julie's essence into some frustrating Tuesday afternoons in your life by just picking up *Hard Curves* and transporting yourself into Julie's very special world.

Hank Rose, 1995
Chairman, Comic Images

Title: Warrior of Light, 1993
Medium: Oil and Acrylic
Size: 15 x 20 in (38 x 51 cm)
Video Game Cover,
Super Nintendo

With commissions like this Julie usually receives a tape of someone playing the game to give an idea of how it works. The visuals are constantly improving but often, as in this case, she is required to translate tiny blots of colour into a realistic image, which in fact is more fun than just sharpening up well-defined characters.

1

Metallic Images

Coming up so fast through the field has been very exciting, but also a bit scary when she remembers how a few years ago the notion of becoming a professional artist was just a lingering but faint dream in the background. Her sons are simply delighted, though, both with the paintings and with her new lifestyle.

Julie ©93

J ulie Bell comes originally from Texas, and although she has lived in many parts of the United States since then, a certain Texan raunchiness lingers in her accent, manner and work. She is no shrinking violet. She holds views which many regard as politically incorrect, but does so with such warmth and generosity of spirit that one can't help wondering whether her critics have any idea what they are talking about.

Her portrayal of women is the most obvious target, and yet when she talks on the subject it soon becomes clear that sexploitation is the last thing on her mind. In her own way she is a staunch feminist, and her paintings aim to project the empowerment and independence of women.

One of the remarkable things about her paintings is the abundance with which she produces them. Most of the pictures in this collection were painted in a period of two or three years; more startling still, this span began only a couple of years after she learned to wield a paintbrush and decided to try her hand at becoming a professional artist. Many people dream of finding an opening where all their energies can combine into a body of work from which they can stand back and feel proud. Fewer rise to the occasion when it presents itself. Here is someone who has done both, and her success owes as much to her talent and determination as to finding herself in the right place at the right time.

In a few short years her superheroes have fought their way on to book and comic

Title: Enchanted Charge, 1993
Medium: Oil and Acrylic
Size: 15 x 20 in (38 x 51 cm)
Cover, Marvel Comics

Although the monster looks a very characteristic Julie Bell creation, it was in fact taken from the comic, which had been illustrated by another artist. This was her first experience of doing this and although in a way it meant her creative input was lessened, injecting dynamism into the scene was demanding enough to make it satisfying.

Title: Prehistoric Metal, 1993
Medium: Oil and Acrylic
Size: 11 x 15 in (28 x 38 cm)
Portfolio Piece

This painting began as a landscape
exercise, the metallic pterodactyl
being added later on a whim. Julie
imagined it as something a football
team might have as a mascot.

Title: Evil Idol, 1993
Medium: Oil and Acrylic
Size: 15 x 20 in (38 x 51 cm)
Cover, Marvel Comics

One of a pair of *Conan* covers
that were the start of a very fruitful
relationship with Marvel Comics,
who admired some previous *Conan*
book covers by Julie so much that
they let her take her pick of
comics to illustrate.

Julie ©93

Title: SemiAutomatic, 1994
Medium: Oil and Acrylic
Size: 11 x 15 in (28 x 38 cm)
Trading Card, SkyBox

Painting created for SkyBox Master
Series™: Creators Edition Trading Cards.
© SkyBox International Inc.

Part of an interesting challenge in which
Julie and four other artists were each
invited to create twenty-one of their own
superheroes to fit the outline of a story.

16 Hard Curves

Title: Goldrop, 1994 ▷
Medium: Oil and Acrylic
Size: 11 x 15 in (28 x 38 cm)
Trading Card, SkyBox

Painting created for SkyBox Master Series™: Creators Edition Trading Cards. © SkyBox International Inc.

There is an interesting tension here between the languid sensuality of the pose and the metallic hardness of the figure.

covers, trading cards, video game covers and many other places. Some are her interpretations of established characters like The Silver Surfer, Iron Man and Colossus, her first three trading-card images for Marvel Comics; and it is particularly satisfying doing portrayals of characters such as Storm who were comic-book favourites years before she dreamed she might be involved with them directly. *Conan the Barbarian* – an interesting challenge for a female artist – was Julie Bell's introduction to book-cover illustration, while promotion work led to commissions for portraits of Lois and Superman from the current TV series and Batman from the third blockbuster movie about the caped crusader.

In addition she has created dozens, if not hundreds, of memorable superheroes of her own; she often just paints when the mood takes her, and some of her most striking and popular images have arisen this way. Enjoyment of her craft is one of the qualities that bring these pictures to life. Another is their sensuously sculptural character, which creates the illusion of the viewer being able to reach in and touch whatever is in the painting. Foreground textures are rendered with a loving care made possible only by a very firm grasp of technique, particularly considering the speed with which the artist works.

A technique she has grasped with a vengeance is the rendering of polished metal, which has become a trademark of her work. This came about almost accidentally, however. The first two metallic paintings were produced as an experimental departure, but then a publisher suggested she create a matching series, and it somehow escalated from there: 'Painting metal has really been good for me, it's opened doors that might otherwise have remained shut.'

The term 'metal flesh' has been coined to express one aspect of her use of metal effect:

Title: Beauty and The Steel Beast, 1990
Medium: Oil and Acrylic
Size: 15 x 20 in (38 x 51 cm)
Portfolio Piece

An example of failure turning to success. The painting was suggested by a friend who models in the music business, with the dual purpose of getting both herself and Julie's work on to an album cover for the Great White group. It turned out that another cover had already been commissioned but in its own right the picture has proved even more successful. It was also Julie's first metallic picture.

Julie ©90

Julie ©91

instead of hard, unyielding steel contrasting
with soft human flesh, the flesh itself
becomes steel and the contrast is
internalized. The result is oddly pleasing,
often subliminal. The strength of steel is
tempered by its implied suppleness; the
vulnerability of flesh takes on the power and
imperviousness of polished metal.

Power is a word Julie Bell uses a fair amount in talking about both life and art: 'I think I've always been really strong inside but for the first thirty years of my life I often let people walk all over me. I didn't know how to stand up for myself. Then I realized I am a really strong person. When you find your power you have to learn to be responsible with it. Power can be used either to hurt or to create, so you have to think of the people around you. But we all have a responsibility to ourselves too. No one should be a doormat.'

Much of this confidence comes from her new-found success as an artist, something which could hardly have been predicted a few years earlier. She had always wanted to be an artist but no way had presented itself, and she had met no-one – except perhaps teachers – who made their living that way. She did a lot of drawing for fun, but the closest she had come to turning professional was doing cartoons for a children's book and training to be a scientific/medical illustrator. Then, in 1989 Julie met the fantasy artist Boris Vallejo through a mutual interest in bodybuilding. They later married.

To Boris she happily gives credit for helping her find her feet. From him she learned not only the technical side of painting but also how to take an idea and turn it into a work of art: 'It was very lucky. There's no way I could have this kind of career without being taught the way I was. The key thing has been confidence. Boris believed in me and could show me the road. Then I learned confidence in my own ability and found clients who shared it.'

Title: Space Cowgirl, 1992
Medium: Oil and Acrylic
Size: 15 x 20 in (38 x 51 cm)
Portfolio Piece

Coming from Texas, Julie has always had a soft spot for cowboys and cowgirls, so the motive for this painting was mainly her own enjoyment. The creature is the way it is just for fun. One can't help wondering whether the ride it can offer will be worth all the effort of saddling it up, but that is part of the entertainment. Julie says she is quite capable of being serious, but not all the time.

Julie©92

Title: First Touch, 1993
Medium: Oil and Acrylic
Size: 15 x 20 in (38 x 51 cm)
Portfolio Piece

Another painting done mainly for
the artist's own satisfaction. The aim
was for a quieter subject than usual,
and to capture something of the
feeling of the 'first time'. Just as,
according to some accounts, there is
only ever one unicorn in existence,
so we all only have one first time.
The lady's attitude teeters between
timidity and determination.

She turned professional in 1991 upon taking some work speculatively
to *Heavy Metal* magazine, where it was greeted with enthusiasm. A
comfortable relationship developed; she takes in paintings she thinks
suitable from time to time, and the magazine usually publishes them.

From this beginning, Julie Bell advanced rapidly into the front rank
of fantasy painters. Coming up so fast has been exciting, but also scary
for someone who until a few years ago was struggling to bring up two
children, the notion of becoming an artist just a faint dream. Her sons
are delighted, both with the paintings and her new lifestyle. They
enjoy pointing out the occasional costume fault in her superheroes and
are turning into very good artists themselves. Having grown up among
superheroes, they hope to produce comics of their own some day.

Title: Wind Rider, 1993
Medium: Oil and Acrylic
Size: 15 x 20 in (38 x 51 cm)
Portfolio Piece

A study in textures and contrasts; flesh,
metal, water, rocks. The artist's aim is
to make these things seem as tangible to
the viewer as if they were in the scene
themselves, and very often she succeeds.

Title: Marble Master, 1993
Medium: Oil and Acrylic
Size: 11 x 15 in (28 x 38 cm)
Portfolio Piece

One of Julie's sons with an infuriated
friend. Julie would love to see a story
made of this, and it would be fascinating
to know why the monster is so helpless
against the kid's quiet confidence. He's
furious about losing the game but cannot
do anything about it, even though by
rights he should be able to bite the boy's
head off without a second thought.

Title: Child's Play, 1993
Medium: Oil and Acrylic
Size: 11 x 15 in (28 x 38 cm)
Trading Card

When doing a set of card illustrations, Julie found herself suddenly needing ten extra paintings, so she turned to her sons for inspiration and asked what they would like to do or be. Here, David adopts a typically dramatic pose. In case you were wondering, his teeth have been exaggerated slightly.

Title: Ecstasy, 1990
Medium: Oil and Acrylic
Size: 11 x 15 in (28 x 38 cm)
Portfolio Piece

A celebration of both rainstorms and sensuality. The aim of much of the artist's work is to promote the idea that it is healthy to have sensual feelings, and to be happy and at peace with one's physicality.

2

Sensuality

At the age of 18 she first took
life drawing classes and found it
enormously exhilarating. For the first time
she really noticed a certain line that runs
down from the male shoulder which
for her is one of the most beautiful lines
in the human form; and she fell in love
with the whole experience of trying to
capture all the planes and muscles of the
human form in two dimensions.

Julie Bell

Sensuality is another word the artist often uses when discussing her work. She tends to think in sensual terms and this translates into how she tackles her paintings. Sensuality to her is a tactile as much as an emotional thing, perhaps even more so. The aim of her pictures is that the viewer should feel almost able to reach in and touch whatever is in them, or at least imagine what it would feel like to be in the scene. Julie Bell herself loves to be out in the wind and rain and any passing thunderstorm, she loves to feel rocks and trees and everything else in nature. She aims in her paintings to share this with viewers, and perhaps even open their senses so that they too will notice such things. And when she has captured a texture to her own satisfaction, she usually emphasizes it through contrast with something totally different.

Title: Suzanne, 1990
Medium: Oil and Acrylic
Size: 20 x 30 in (51 x 76 cm)
Portfolio Piece

The artist's first real painting, with one of her sisters as a model. It was also the sister's first experience of modelling. The theme arose because Suzanne has always loved horses and relates very well to all animals and nature in general.

As an individual she feels strongly that people are not taught enough how to experience life from a sensual point of view. The pressure in fact is to cover up such feelings. So as an artist she aims to redress the balance as far as possible and celebrate the sensual side of life. She aims to show that it is healthy and leads to being in control of your life – as are the subjects of her paintings, who are virtually always shown as masters of their circumstances.

Often the effect is achieved by her characters' expressions. She likes to show people absorbed in what they are doing, lost in their own world of pleasure. It may come from the lines of the composition. S-shaped curves tend to convey a sensual message, not

Title: Golden Lover, 1992
Medium: Oil and Acrylic
Size: 15 x 20 in (38 x 51 cm)
Portfolio Piece

Sometimes ideas arise from photographs of a subject but in this case the idea came first and the model posed accordingly. The feeling Julie wanted to get across was of the two having some kind of love relationship despite their obvious differences. It was her first use of gold metal, which she realized has a much warmer quality than silver, though for the sake of contrast this is not always desirable. The serpent's soft, flowing fins do much to make the relationship credible. If they were hard and spiky the effect would be totally different.

just in the main figures but in the whole composition. If the key elements are linked with sensual curves, that is the subliminal message that comes across, just as harsh, jagged lines create a climate of violence.

Power is also an element in some of these sensual pictures: 'Kissinger said that power is the greatest aphrodisiac. It took me a long time to understand that it works two ways. It

Title: Serpent Sage, 1990
Medium: Oil and Acrylic
Size: 15 x 20 cm (38 x 51 in)
Portfolio Piece

An early painting from before the artist learned how to paint metal, or the serpent may well have acquired at least a metallic sheen. One of the attractions of fantasy is the freedom of being able to depict sexuality in these terms.

Title: Spider Whisper, 1993
Medium: Oil and Acrylic
Size: 11 x 15 in (28 x 38 cm)
Portfolio Piece

Derived from a photograph in Boris Vallejo's collection, this painting began as a figure study in 1990 when the artist was first learning to paint. Later she returned and reworked it with the confidence she had acquired in the meantime. The relationship between the spider and the woman remains an enigma. Obviously there is some kind of intimacy but what the whisper is about is left to the imagination of the viewer.

Title: Hallucin, 1994
Medium: Oil and Acrylic
Size: 11 x 15 in (28 x 38 cm)
Trading Card, SkyBox

Painting created for SkyBox
Master Series™. Creator's Edition
Trading Cards. ©1995 SkyBox
International Inc.

As suggested by her name, this
character has the power of creating
wild and vivid illusions, and does so
with complete and calm confidence.
Julie Bell's fantasy women may share
the almost nonexistent costume
of others in the genre, but they are
always in control of themselves
and their circumstances.

Title: The Sorceress' Flower, 1992
Medium: Oil and Acrylic
Size: 15 x 20 in (38 x 51 cm)
Portfolio Piece

The title can sometimes make all the
difference to a painting. In this case, if it
was called 'Dreaming Maiden About to
be Ravaged by a Monster', that is how
it would appear. As it is, the monster
is clearly spellbound and powerless.

The aim was to capture a feeling of mutual power. The characters enhance each other's individual power through the magical dance they are performing to bring the tattoo to life. The idea was suggested by a Boris Vallejo painting.

is an aphrodisiac to the person with the power, but also to the person with that person. People are attracted to power. A lot of my paintings have that kind of feeling.' But she is not talking about domination. Julie Bell's maidens do not wilt into the arms of her barbarian heroes. Half their attraction is that they too are powerful and free.

Sexuality is an element of these sensual pictures, but not in the way many people imagine at first glance. These are not, or hardly ever, sexual fantasies; they are less personal than that. They are fantasy paintings that often express and celebrate sexuality – and there is a difference. With female figures it is celebrated from within, with male ones from the outside, but always from a slight distance. There is not meant to be anything gloating or prurient about these pictures; if that is the impression of the viewer it is, in the artist's opinion, the viewer's own problem.

In the end Julie Bell just loves the human form, male and female, and does not suffer from any sense of primness. Her attitude is partly the result of an abiding interest in bodybuilding, which explains also why her subjects tend to have such well-toned physiques, but fundamentally it is simply part of her character.

Her general interest in art dates back to childhood. At school she showed a definite flair for art and was always drawing comic books, tattoos on friends and people in costume. These pictures were always basically portraits and were often a useful way of supplementing her pocket money, as the other kids frequently paid her for them. Even in those days she enjoyed the challenge of capturing a likeness and, equally, getting a mood across.

Julie ©92

38 Hard Curves

JuGe©93

In the fifth grade the class was asked: 'What
is your goal in life?' When the question
reached the young Julie Bell, she was lost for
an immediate reply. Then, after a pause that
was to prove prophetic, since it would be a
long time till it came true, she said: 'OK
then, I'll be an artist.'

At the age of eighteen she first took life
drawing classes and found it enormously
exhilarating. Her first model was a male
ballet dancer who was not particularly large
or muscular but was wonderfully fit and
supple. For the first time she really noticed a
certain line that runs down from the male
shoulder which for her is one of the most
beautiful lines in the human form; and she
fell in love with the whole experience of
trying to capture all the planes and muscles
of the human form in two dimensions.

There was little chance to do much about
it, however. At university she took art classes
but then married early, to a professor who
moved around different colleges, so the
chance of going to art school never arose.

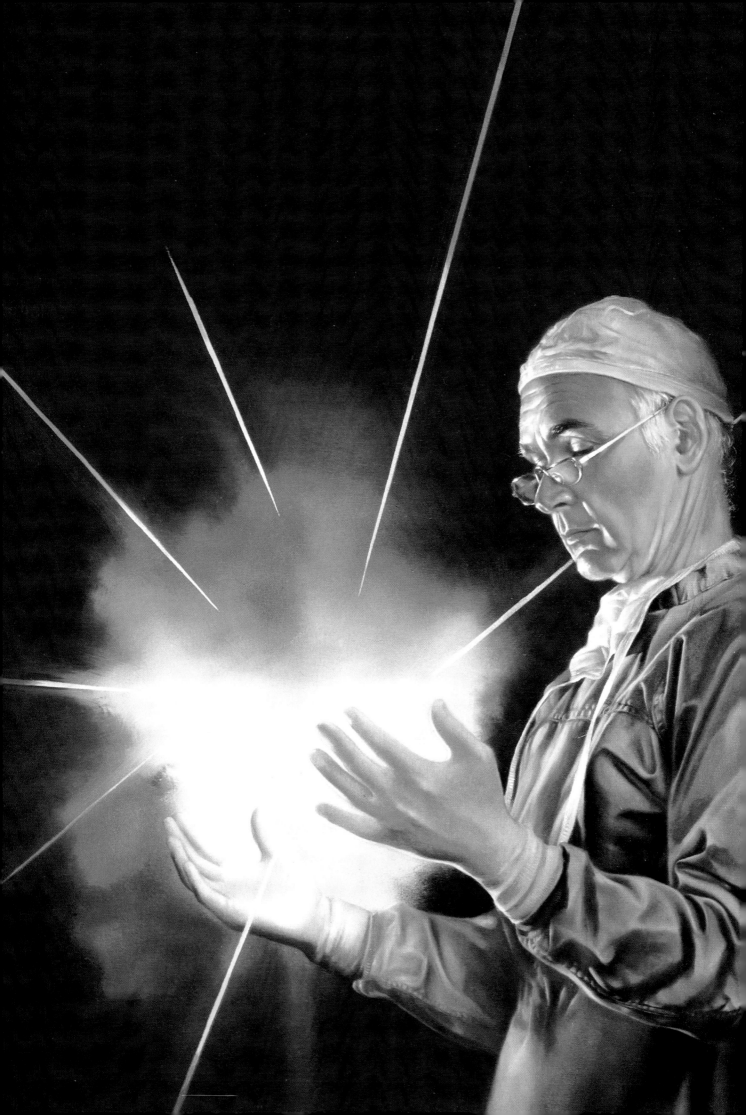

3

Portraits

Some of the models are professionals,
often the artist poses herself or uses
members of her immediate family, and
sometimes they are friends or
acquaintances. Finding volunteers is
rarely a problem. Most people leap at the
chance and often display surprising aspects
of character once they are in costume or
in the mood of a part. Very few people
have refused, and everyone who has
tried it has enjoyed the experience.

Some of the portraits in this chapter are of real individuals, some are of fictional characters, and some are a combination of the two. According to Julie, 'The main thing about a true portrait is to capture both the likeness and the spirit of the subject, and I feel disappointed when I feel I haven't done that, sometimes because there is not the time. A good likeness in itself is not enough. There are a lot of tiny details in a person's face and body language that make you see what that person is, clues to their character.

Portrait of Julie by Maya Vallejo

In faces just the slightest change in the eyebrows, the set of the jaw and so on change the character and emotion in the face. They reflect the spirit of the subject. A likeness without the spirit just looks like a mannequin of the subject.

'With portraits of TV or sports personalities I often have only someone else's photographs to work from, which is a challenge and can be hard. You can't change the pose or safely imagine what the person would look like from another angle.'

Often also she receives only head shots of her subjects, which means trying to imagine the rest and finding a model to fit that idea,

◁ *Title:* Dr Flash, 1992
Medium: Oil and Acrylic
Size: 15 x 20 in (38 x 51 cm)
Britton Advertising

An enjoyable commission since the artist was at one time training as a medical illustrator. The model was her children's doctor, who was delighted to be asked, and with the result. This was the first time she had used this kind of background special effect, which was quite scary as the main figure had already been completed.

Title: Strong As Steel, 1994 ▷
Medium: Oil and Acrylic
Size: 15 x 20 in (38 x 51 cm)
Portfolio Piece

A symbolic self-portrait painted mainly because it had been a while since the last one, also as a sample for a set of cards. The creature on the flag captures the artist's ideal of strength without aggression. The floating rock is also important. It's not that Julie is or wants to be isolated too much of the time, but she believes that to find your inner strength you sometimes need to be alone.

then grafting the two together. Everything different is a challenge and usually it works, but it can feel like operating under a handicap.

The way Julie Bell usually operates is to invite models to the photographic studio she shares with Boris Vallejo and take a large number of photographs from which she chooses a few on which to base her paintings. Sometimes the models are posed with a particular end in mind, sometimes they are just fired up and the resulting shots themselves suggest ideas for paintings.

Drawing or painting directly from posed models is something the artist still loves but rarely has the chance for because the result is too static for most of the work she does: 'Plus it would be really expensive. When taking photographs you can get more exciting poses, expressions and so on. It's far more spontaneous and also great fun. Most of the poses I use in my pictures would be impossible to hold for any length of time. Some are impossible anyway because they're exaggerated and would break your back if you tried them.'

Some of the models are professionals, often the artist poses herself or uses members of her immediate family, and sometimes they are friends or acquaintances. Finding volunteers is rarely a problem.

Title: Spike, 1994
Medium: Oil and Acrylic
Size: 11 x 15 in (28 x 38 cm)
Trading Card, SkyBox

Painting created for SkyBox Master Series™. Creator's Edition Trading Cards.
© 1995 SkyBox International Inc.

The artist modelled for this herself, exercising a side of her character that does not show very often. But it's good, she says, to be reminded that it's still there if it needs to be called on.

Most people leap at the chance and often display surprising aspects of character once they are in costume or in the mood of a part. Very few people have refused, and everyone who has tried it has enjoyed the experience. Modelling and role-playing seem to release an energy that many people are not aware of till they try it, and the artist finds that people seem to value themselves in a different way afterwards; their self-image changes. They feel good about it afterwards too, especially when they see the finished painting.

'Whatever model comes here, I first try to get a feel of their personality, style and so on.

Title: Lilandra, 1993
Medium: Oil and Acrylic
Size: 11 x 15 in (28 x 38 cm)
Trading Card, Marvel Comics

The artist modelled for this herself but did not aim for a close likeness as she has found superheroes work best with a slightly impersonal look.

Title: Murraya, 1994
Medium: Oil and Acrylic
Size: 11 x 15 in (28 x 38 cm)
Trading Card, SkyBox

Painting created for SkyBox Master Series™. Creator's Edition Trading Cards.
© 1995 SkyBox International Inc.

A portrait of Linda Murray, Ms Olympia in the bodybuilding world. One modelling session with her yielded five or six paintings of which the artist is proud, rather than the usual one or two. 'She has a really exotic face and I wanted this portrait to look as much like her as I could make it. I feel she has the spirit of an artist, but I don't know her well enough to be sure of that.'

Title: Creatures of the Woods, 1990
Medium: Oil and Acrylic
Size: 15 x 20 in (38 x 51 cm)
Portfolio Piece

One of the artist's first fantasy paintings. Her two sons were models and she loved the way they came out. With hindsight she wishes she had made the creature fiercer on the principle that 'If you're going to paint a scary monster, it should be supremely bad or else you lose the tension of opposites.'

Title: Kat's Pet, 1990
Medium: Oil and Acrylic
Size: 15 x 20 in (38 x 51 cm)
Portfolio piece

The artist's first painting of this sister, and the first time her sister had ever modelled, an experience she loved. The beast and the setting were chosen to illustrate, in fantasy terms, a certain resilience of character in the subject.

Title: Steel Wings, 1993
Medium: Oil and Acrylic
Size: 15 x 20 in (38 x 51 cm)
Portfolio Piece

Another symbolic self-portrait, showing an awakening to power over life. The feathers turning into birds are how Julie sees her paintings, flying off into the world and acquiring a life of their own, rather like children. Within the context of the painting she imagined the birds eventually growing into winged females too.

I like doing caricatures, picking what really stands out in their personality or the way they move. Each person has something different to offer and I don't try to force them to do what doesn't suit them. I don't make a cheerful person try to look serious or the other way round. Sometimes I choose a model to fit a character I have in mind, sometimes I create a character to suit the model, it varies.'

Portraits 49

Not a standard superhero portrait
because it is an unusual character.
The absence of action meant having
to try and capture the nature of the
detective with body language.

Reference photographs are also sometimes used for backgrounds but more loosely than with the main figures: 'It's really good to work from reference, but you can't be a slave to it. You make your own drawing and just use the reference to fill in the details to add genuineness.'

Monsters are obviously trickier to find either models or reference material for: 'It's scarier painting something totally created, going totally from your own judgement. With photographs you can tell when a painting is finished but there's an insecurity with something you've just imagined. Usually it takes time to distance yourself and see it objectively.'

Something she learned early on when painting skin tones was not to think too much in terms of 'flesh' colours. The more different shades there are, the more life there is to the picture. Sometimes she has set out deliberately to paint flesh in really strange colours to give the figure a non-human look, but it still looks human anyway because the mind just assumes the lighting is strange.

When composing a picture, one of the first decisions is about how it is going to relate to the viewer. In an action scene, if any character makes eye contact with the viewer it creates a dynamic and pulls the viewer into the picture. It has to be decided if the tension is going to be between the characters, or between the characters and the viewer: 'A lot of times it's easier to enter the picture if there is no eye contact. There's a voyeuristic tendency like when you're watching TV. If the character's looking straight at you, it can hold

Title: Lois with Cape, 1994
Medium: Oil and Acrylic
Size: 11 x 15 in (28 x 38 cm)
Publicity, DC Comics/Warner Brothers

Trademarked and copyrighted © 1995
DC Comics. All rights reserved.

With a character as well established as this there is not much room for an illustrator to improvise, but more is required than a simple copy of the photographic reference provided. To inject life into the picture it needs to be enhanced minutely here and there.

Title: Lois & Superman, 1994
Medium: Oil and Acrylic
Size: 11 x 15 in (28 x 38 cm)
Publicity, DC Comics/
Warner Brothers

you back. Also you have to decide how much
to put in and what to leave out. It's good to
leave a gap of mystery in a picture which the
viewer can fill with their own imagination,
and so make the picture partly their own.'

There is a saying that you cannot have a
good movie without a villain, and as a general
rule she has found the same with paintings.
Some tension of opposites is usually required.

Titles are something the artist gives a lot of thought to as well, even knowing that many people pay no attention to them. She does it, however, for those who do take notice, and occasionally they are for her quite crucial for a picture to make sense.

One criticism Julie Bell has faced, and occasionally overheard at shows when people have not known she was nearby, is that her paintings look too much like Boris Vallejo's. Any criticism can sting, particularly when you pay as much attention to audience comments as the artist does, but it is not really something she feels defensive about: 'Boris and I agree in so many aspects, we like so many of the same things, so why should our art not be similar as well? Also he taught me to paint. If I'd learned from Leonardo or Michelangelo my paintings would probably have ended up looking like theirs. Would it matter?

Boris Vallejo in a frisky mood. 'He has a great sense of humour and is not at all afraid to play up to the camera. He also makes a great model because he knows exactly what I'm looking for.'

Technique counts in art, and particularly in illustration. It also helps to be shown how to organize your ideas and to be pointed in the direction of the right doors to knock on when looking for work. But all this counts for nothing if you have no imagination, which is something that cannot be taught. There are ways in which it can be encouraged and nurtured but basically you either have it or you don't. What Boris has done is show Julie ways in which to express her imagination and become the artist she always wanted to be.

It helped that she had stayed pretty much away from painting before she met him

Title: Robo Vampire, 1992
Medium: Oil and Acrylic
Size: 11 x 15 in (28 x 38 cm)
Portfolio Piece

Based on a photograph in Boris' own collection. The aim was to capture his more mysterious, dark side.

Julie ©94

The artist has always loved American Indian art,
attitudes and way of life, and this chance of
creating a superhero character seemed a good
opportunity to express something along those
lines. It also seemed a good moment for another
portrait of Boris Vallejo who, coming from Peru,
has a good deal of South American Indian in him
and embodies the ideal for Julie in other ways: 'He
has an incredibly strong face and presence and
gives a feeling of being a very solid person. I
wanted to show his strength and passion.'

because there were no preconceived ideas to unlearn. In school she
experimented with acrylic landscapes and in college she studied
colour and design theory, which comes in useful today, but she stayed
away from painting with oils. For some reason she was afraid of them
and had no idea how to begin handling them.

Many illustrators aspire to working in oils but don't on the grounds
that they take too long to dry. Julie Bell has not found this a problem,
though, and as she produces her paintings at a furious rate it
obviously is not. Two to three days is quite normal for her to take a
painting from start to finish, a rate achieved partly by using only
turpentine, not linseed oil, for thinning the paint; she also applies the
paint quite thinly, which she prefers anyway, as with thick paint it is
much harder to get the colours right.

Not least of the reasons the artist enjoys oil paints is the way they
smell. And she likes the way backgrounds can be almost sculpted by
laying it on quite freely and then 'pulling' it away with turps,
resulting in a very spontaneous look for rocks and other natural
things: 'You have to learn the balance between when to control what

An enigmatic study of light and shade, in both colour and mood.

Title: To Become A Man, 1990
Medium: Oil and Acrylic
Size: 11 x 15 in (28 x 38 cm)
Portfolio Piece

What the artist enjoys about using her son Tony as a model is that he is not afraid to show his sensitive side and can address the camera very honestly. He loves entering into roles like this and has the ability to get completely lost in the part.

60 **Hard Curves**

Title: Rescue, 1991

Medium: Oil and Acrylic

Size: 15 x 20 in (38 x 51 cm)

Portfolio Piece

A sample painting produced to tempt
commissions in a similar vein, such as
an illustrated *Arabian Nights*. It has not
happened yet but the artist remains
open to offers, as everyone had great
fun dressing up for the part.

you're doing and when to let the painting have its own life. Too much control makes the picture too stifled.'

The same applies when trying out new special effects. The temptation is to be cautious but she find that without courage the effect tends to get toned down to the point where nothing happens. Curiously, this freestyle approach to painting natural things applies equally to painting weird and wonderful machinery or banks of computers. It is far more spontaneous than people imagine.

The normal procedure with a painting is to start with a pencil sketch on primed illustration board. This is then fleshed out with an acrylic foundation; oils could be used at this stage but take longer to

Title: Young Wizard, 1990
Medium: Oil and Acrylic
Size: 11 x 15 in (28 x 38 cm)
Portfolio Piece

One of the artist's first fantasy paintings, which began with Julie's son David posing as the Statue of Liberty but somehow evolved into this.

Title: Skito Bite, 1994

Medium: Oil and Acrylic

Size: 11 x 15 in (28 x 38 cm)

Trading Card, SkyBox

Painting created for SkyBox Master Series™. Creator's Edition Trading Cards. © 1995 SkyBox International Inc.

A superhero character dreamed up by the model, the artist's son David, who sheds all inhibitions in front of the camera.

Title: Junior Seau, 1994
Medium: Oil and Acrylic
Size: 11 x 15 in (28 x 38 cm)
Trading Card, NFL/Playoff
Courtesy of NFL Quarterback Club, Inc.

Part of a really interesting project depicting
football stars as superheroes, which they
are to many people since they are capable
of almost superhuman feats of skill.

Title: Barry Sanders, 1994
Medium: Oil and Acrylic
Size: 11 x 15 in (28 x 38 cm)
Trading Card, NFL/Playoff
Courtesy of NFL
Quarterback Club, Inc.

A blue lion is the
player's team mascot.

Title: Marcus Allen, 1994
Medium: Oil and Acrylic
Size: 11 x 15 in (28 x 38 cm)
Trading Card, NFL/Playoff
Courtesy of National Football
League Players Association.

This player is a veteran who returned
to the game from retirement, hence
the phoenix. The artist also wanted
to give his portrait something of
the quality of an Indian chief as a
token of his experience.

dry. The result is a more or less brown and
white version of the picture's main features,
details being left for the final stage to allow
spontaneity. Then comes the oil painting.

It all sounds quite simple put like that.
Obviously there is a lot more to it but the
details of her technique are not something
the artist particularly wishes to expand on, as
painting is such a non-verbal occupation and
also what works for one artist does not
necessarily work for another. What counts is
the result. And when she has a result Julie
loves to get opinions from everybody who is
interested, whether they are artists or not, on

Title: Emmitt Smith, 1994
Medium: Oil and Acrylic
Size: 11 x 15 in (28 x 38 cm)
Trading Card, NFL/Playoff
Courtesy of NFL
Quarterback Club, Inc.

Smith was a trophy winner the
year this was painted, hence his
depiction as Atlas. He is also a
very happy, exuberant character,
which has been captured well.

the principle that how people see a picture is
as important as how she would like them to
see it, maybe even more so.

A curious experience for her is when
people like a painting which she feels is a
failure: 'But you're never completely satisfied
anyway. Every picture falls short of what you
imagine, you can never get all the details
right. It's like trying to remember a
wonderful dream. The same thing happens to
Boris. There are some of his pictures that I
like which aren't at all as he intended.'

Title: Sterling Sharpe, 1994
Medium: Oil and Acrylic
Size: 11 x 15 in (28 x 38 cm)
Trading Card, NFL/Playoff
Courtesy of National Football
League Players Association.

This player has a reputation
for ploughing through the field
like a machine, so was
presented as a machine.

Superheroes

The appeal of superhero women is that they are beautiful and go around virtually naked but, even if they were real, they would be beyond reach. You can look but not touch. In a way their paint-thin costumes raise a barrier of propriety so you can look at them without crossing the boundary that nakedness often creates.

Julie ©92

The attraction of painting superheroes for Julie Bell is that their costumes are basically just painted skin, so they are really figure studies. Also they are often flying or involved in greatly exaggerated action: 'One of the things in general about superheroes is that you're aiming to capture energy and movement, or "muscles in motion" as they say in the trade. I learned a lot from illustrating video games where the first expression of the characters gives a feeling of what is happening. In this kind of picture it's often useful to have the characters off-balance so if they really stood the way you paint them, they'd fall over. It creates a tension that feeds often subliminally to the viewer.'

The first of these superheroes the
artist created for Skybox, using one
of her sisters as a model. To create
the sense of movement, the character
is totally off-balance, an effect
heightened by the stiletto heels.

One of the artist's favourite paintings.
The character looks like she can conquer
the universe; she is exposed but at the
same time totally untouchable.

A feature of most comic covers is that
the characters come bursting out of them
towards the viewer to grab attention. Most
trading cards use the same technique: 'It's a
one-shot thing, unlike the inside of a comic
where there is a story to tell and there is
room for a variety of moods.'

Alternatively, in both comics and trading
cards it is sometimes decided to go for an
action scene in which the viewer is not
directly involved. Often the client decides
in advance which of the two main
approaches is to be taken.

A basic feature of superheroes is that their
bodies are more perfect than ever occurs in
real life. Even when using bodybuilders as

Title: Swamp, 1994
Medium: Oil and Acrylic
Size: 15 x 20 in (38 x 51 cm)
Trading Card, SkyBox

Painting created for SkyBox
Master Series™. Creator's Edition
Trading Cards. © 1995 SkyBox
International, Inc.

Most trading cards have information
about the characters on the back, but
for a change some carried this scene
broken down into nine parts. Because
there are no main figures in the
painting, elements like the buildings
were sharpened up more than usual.

models, they need to be idealized. In the artist's opinion this is why
it is so hard to make good superhero movies without using padded
costumes: 'In these paintings you have to remember the difference
between fantasy and reality. If I just took photographs and painted
them, it would fail. You have to imagine the characters as seven foot
tall to give them the right quality. Even in terms of pose you have to
exaggerate. When shooting pictures I can never quite get the energy
from one photo. You have to piece the thing together from a variety
of shots. There's no way you can get most of these poses anyway, the
looseness would break a normal person's hips and spine and so on.'

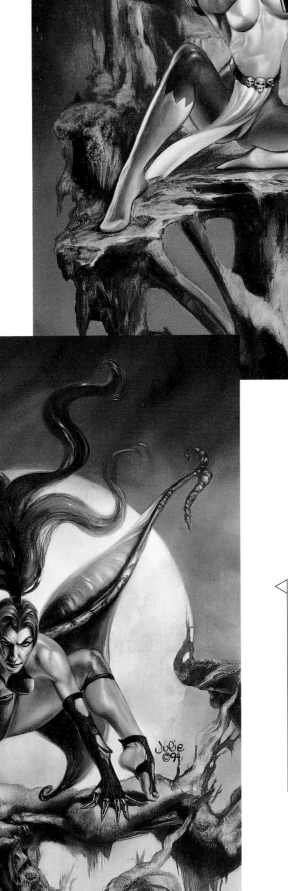

Title: Mystique, 1994
Medium: Oil and Acrylic
Size: 11 x 15 in (28 x 38 cm)
Trading Card, Marvel Comics

Title: Sparrow, 1994
Medium: Oil and Acrylic
Size: 11 x 15 in (28 x 38 cm)
Trading Card, SkyBox

Painting created for SkyBox
Master Series™. Creator's Edition
Trading Cards. © 1995 SkyBox
International, Inc.

The aim was for a kind of human
vampire moth. The original
painting was given to the Art
Director at SkyBox as a present.

Title: White Queen, 1990

Medium: Oil and Acrylic

Size: 11 x 15 in (28 x 38 cm)

Trading Card, Marvel Comics

Copyright © 1995 Marvel
Entertainment Group, Inc.
All rights reserved.

A dangerous lady. Her dress and
manner are inviting but you know
she'll keep total control of any
situation and is basically untouchable.

Title: Princess Mustang, 1994

Medium: Oil and Acrylic

Size: 11 x 15 in (28 x 38 cm)

Trading Card, SkyBox

Painting created for SkyBox Master
Series™. Creator's Edition Trading Cards.
© 1995 SkyBox International, Inc.

In contrast to the White Queen, this
character looks nice, even emotionally
vulnerable. The difference has little to do
with costume and everything to do with
facial expression and body language.

A growing trend is for the artist to use
people who go in for fitness competitions
rather than bodybuilding as models.
Part of the aim of fitness training is to
develop muscles, but looking good in a
bikini counts for more and to some
eyes the ladies are more 'feminine'.

One of the artist's favourite comic
characters shown just having fun
flying above the city. Rogue is a
slightly ambivalent character, having
started out on the side of the bad
guys and changed over.

One thing she learned early on was that
when portraying battles between heroes and
villains, 'the bad guys have to be much bigger
and more dangerous-looking, otherwise the
heroes can end up looking like bullies.'

The appeal of many superhero women, the
artist believes, is that they are beautiful and go
around virtually naked but, even if they were
real, they would be beyond reach. You can look
but not touch. In a way their paint-thin costumes
make them sexier than if they were naked, but
the costumes raise a barrier of propriety so you
can look at them without crossing the boundary
that nakedness often creates.

Although working within a genre, Julie has
her own rules about what she will or will not

Title: C.L.I.P., 1994 ▷
Medium: Oil and Acrylic
Size: 11 x 15 in (28 x 38 cm)
Trading Card, SkyBox

Painting created for SkyBox
Master Series™. Creator's Edition
Trading Cards. © 1995 SkyBox
International, Inc.

Both Julie's sons are allowed
to suggest characters occasionally,
on the condition that she
can modify them in any way
she chooses, as she knows the
constraints and requirements
better. With certain modifications
(including, as it happens, a change
of sex) this character was the
creation of her son Tony.

do. For instance, a lot of artists in this area of fantasy dwell on their characters' more painful moments, she never does. Fear, tension, danger and adventure are fine, but not suffering. Not for the heroes, anyway; monsters and villains take an occasional beating.

Contrasts of all kinds appeal to the artist – good/bad, cold/hot, hard/soft. The contrast of metal and flesh is the one for which she is best known, and although she has explored it in many different ways the possibilities still seem endless.

People often assume some special kind of silver or gold paint is employed for metal, but in fact it is the same oil paint as everything else in her paintings: 'What you have to realize is that shiny metal is simply a reflection of what's around it, as with water. How to draw

Title: Void, 1994
Medium: Oil and Acrylic
Size: 11 x 15 in (28 x 38 cm)
Trading Card, Image Comics

One of the artist's favourite characters. 'I still think it's funny to see a real person in metal; they're naked but it's alright to look. And with soft metal there is an inbuilt contrast, it's hard and soft at the same time. The effect is a bit like mercury. Some people call it "metal flesh".'

Title: Storm, 1993
Medium: Oil and Acrylic
Size: 11 x 15 in (28 x 38 cm)
Trading Card: Marvel Comics

A very successful painting, a copy of which was spotted painted on to a van in Chicago. At a show the artist also met someone with a tattoo of the design and felt it an enormous compliment that someone wanted to incorporate her work into their lives that way.

Title: Storm II, 1994
Medium: Oil and Acrylic
Size: 11 x 15 in (28 x 38 cm)
Trading Card, Marvel Comics

When reading comics years before turning professional, the artist fell in love with this character through a shared love of storms and flying: so it was an especial pleasure to paint her and incorporate an element of self-portrait. The sensual experience Storm is plainly having here captures well how the artist feels in the same circumstances.

or paint water always fascinated me as a kid. Often when painting metal I think of water, the main difference being that water is partly transparent.

'If you want to paint metal, the thing is to study metal objects and photos. Most important is to look at how others have painted it, to understand what makes things look metallic when translated into 2-D. Often you have to fake a little because what you're dealing with is an illusion really. The aim is to convince the brain it is looking at metal, not just to copy the way metallic objects really do look.

Superheroes 85

'Basically what happens is you get the cooler colours at the top and the warmer ones at the bottom. Sometimes you have to cheat by adding colours that wouldn't really be there, to make the object stand out. Of course, you also have to indicate reflections of whatever's around the object, and lines have to be fluid. They curve around as water does when pulled by surface tension. Working seams into the surface also adds to the effect, which can be

Title: Fire Cat, 1994
Medium: Oil and Acrylic
Size: 11 x 15 in (28 x 38 cm)
Trading Card SkyBox
Painting created for SkyBox
Master Series™. Creator's
Edition Trading Cards. © 1995
SkyBox International, Inc.

Another totally wild painting for
which Boris Vallejo was the model.

◁ *Title:* Gambit, 1994
Medium: Oil and Acrylic
Size: 11 x 15 in (28 x 38 cm)
Trading Card, Marvel Comics

◁ *Title:* Domino, 1994
Medium: Oil and Acrylic
Size: 11 x 15 in (28 x 38 in)
Trading Card, Marvel Comics

Title: Batman, 1993 ▷
Medium: Oil and Acrylic
Size: 15 x 20 in (38 x 51 cm)
Publicity, DC Comics/
Warner Brothers

Possibly the artist's first montage
painting, using film-poster styling for
a magazine to promote the 1995
Batman film. It was an interesting
challenge and Julie had a good time
with it. Since *Batman* is too cool to
smile, she was afraid this might lead
to a still composition but is very
happy with the way it turned out.

Title: Forge, 1993 ▷
Medium: Oil and Acrylic
Size: 11 x 15 in (28 x 38 cm)
Trading Card, Marvel Comics

The setting was inspired by a
scene in the film *Bladerunner.*

Title: Swamp Lord, 1994 ▷
Medium: Oil and Acrylic
Size: 11 x 15 in (28 x 38 cm)
Trading Card, SkyBox

Painting created for SkyBox
Master Series™. Creator's Edition
Trading Cards. © 1995 SkyBox
International, Inc.

A rare example of a Julie Bell
superhero at rest, something she feels
she would not want to do all the
time, but it makes a pleasant change.

Title: Archangel, 1994 ▷
Medium: Oil and Acrylic
Size: 11 x 15 in (28 x 38 cm)
Trading Card, Marvel Comics
Copyright © Marvel Entertainment
Group, Inc. All rights reserved.

Archangel is fighting a monster that
is invisible except by reflection,
as in the shiny wings.

strengthened further by contrasting the metal with some totally different texture.'

Patient and careful study is the basis of the artist's facility with metal effects; and she does things with them that are hard both to explain and to pinpoint. Usually metal looks cold but occasionally she succeeds in heating it up in appearance and even giving it a sensual look. Sometimes the metal seems hard, sometimes as liquid as mercury, and in practice this is all achieved by imagination.

Having grasped the principles of how it is done, Julie Bell works out the reflections in her head. Even if it were possible to set up polished metallic models of whatever she has in mind, she would resist doing so because the effects she achieves without models are more dramatic. She does, however, keep a lot of metal hanging around the studio for inspiration.

The artist's introduction to comic covers was a commission for a couple of Conan pictures from Marvel Comics. These were well received but when she expressed interest

Title: Parasite, 1994
Medium: Oil and Acrylic
Size: 11 x 15 in (28 x 38 cm)
Trading Card, SkyBox

Painting created for SkyBox Master Series™. Creator's Edition Trading Cards. © 1995 SkyBox International, Inc.

This character was created by the artist's son David.

Title: Wolverine, 1994
Medium: Oil and Acrylic
Size: 11 x 15 in (28 x 38 cm)
Trading Card, Marvel Comics

Copyright © Marvel Entertainment Group Inc. All rights reserved

Another ambivalent character who happens to be on the side of good but is very much enjoying smashing things up here.

in doing some superhero trading cards there was less enthusiasm. She was just one of many artists visiting the art director in question and she encountered a distinct lack of confidence. Being female probably did not help as there are very few women artists in this line of work. Reluctantly it was agreed to give her a chance and the requirements were outlined.

When she returned shortly with paintings of the Iron Man, Silver Surfer and Colossus, everyone was stunned because they were perfect: 'But artists have to give publishers a break because they really don't know what you're capable of in advance. They also have deadlines.'

Title: Psylocke II, 1994
Medium: Oil and Acrylic
Size: 11 x 15 in (28 x 38 cm)
Trading Card, Marvel Comics

Being female herself gives her an edge, Julie believes, because she can empathize with the characters from within, unlike most artists in this field.

Title: Psylocke I, 1993
Medium: Oil and Acrylic
Size: 11 x 15 in (28 x 38 cm)
Trading Card, Marvel Comics

The artist's first female character for Marvel, who really liked the way she handled the subject and afterwards put many more females her way.

Title: Jean Gray I, 1994

Medium: Oil and Acrylic

Size: 11 x 15 in (28 x 38 cm)

Trading Card, Marvel Comics

The character is a very graceful one who always
keeps her composure. In capturing her mood it
helps that the artist studied ballet as a child and
learned that every part of the body contributes
to the mood you are trying to express. Even
hands, fingers and toes play a vital part.

Title: Jean Gray II, 1994

Medium: Oil and Acrylic

Size: 11 x 15 in (28 x 38 cm)

Trading Card, Marvel Comics

Jean Gray is under stress here,
but as far as possible the lines of
the picture are still graceful.

Title: Vampirella, 1994 ▷
Medium: Oil and Acrylic
Size: 11 x 15 in (28 x 38 cm)
Trading Card, Harris Comics/
The Topps Company
Vampirella® 2nd © 1995.
Harris Publications, Inc. All
rights reserved. Commissioned
by The Topps Co. Inc.

The artist really loves the feeling
of being outdoors in the woods at
night, and this was a chance to
express much of that. When
looking at it now, she can almost
feel the wind and hard ground.

It felt very good to Julie to prove herself against the odds
and from that point on she launched into a whole series,
several series in fact, of trading-card images for Marvel
and other companies. These included many characters of
her own creation, around which storylines are being
worked for comics and computer games. Creating and
illustrating original storylines is an area of work that Julie
hopes to become much more involved with; she has
several possible stories suitable for comics in mind,
although whether she would feel up to illustrating one
throughout has yet to be put to the test.

Title: Ember, 1994
Medium: Oil and Acrylic
Size: 11 x 15 in (28 x 38 cm)
Trading Card, Skybox

Painting created for SkyBox
Master Series™. Creator's
Edition Trading Cards. © 1995
SkyBox International, Inc.

Not a human figure but the
personification of one of the
elements of a distant planet.

Title: Tempest, 1994
Medium: Oil and Acrylic
Size: 11 x 15 in (28 x 38 cm)
Trading Card, SkyBox

Painting created for SkyBox
Master Series™. Creator's
Edition Trading Cards. © 1995
SkyBox International, Inc.

The personification of Air
who has transmuted a piece of
wind into living metal.

Title: Locus 1993
Medium: Oil and Acrylic
Size: 11 x 15 in (28 x 38 cm)
Trading Card, Marvel Comics

Title: Yrial, 1993
Medium: Oil and Acrylic
Size: 11 x 15 in (28 x 38 cm)
Trading Card, Malibu Comics

The setting is Arizona, which is Julie
Bell's secret or sacred place, where she
goes when she really needs to clear
her mind. Whether she would choose
to live there all the time is another
matter because for many reasons she
wants to live near New York, but
it is an occasional dream.

Title: Shard, 1993
Medium: Oil and Acrylic
Size: 11 x 15 in (28 x 38 cm)
Trading Card, Marvel Comics

Often when painting an established character it is hard to find a suitable model. In this case it was all right but sometimes a blend has to be made from photographs of four or five different subjects.

Title: Dead Eye, 1994
Medium: Oil and Acrylic
Size: 11 x 15 in (28 x 38 cm)
Trading Card, Skybox

Chances to do cheerful characters are quite rare in this line of work so it was a pleasure when this one came along, particularly as this kind of jaunty pose best suited the model. For the uninitiated, dead-eye is an expression for someone who can shoot straight.

One of the artist's favourite
SkyBox paintings, whose aim was
to capture the feeling of as much
strength as possible; so, really hard
metal, really hard muscles but
with a contrast of creamy skin.

Being a specialist in painting
metal is an advantage when it comes
to securing certain commissions.

102 Hard Curves

Painting a robot body like this is
often quicker than a real figure
study as there is more leeway with
the proportions, and it is more
spontaneous than it looks.

All of this is the more exciting because the
artist used to read a lot of comics long before
she thought she might ever do this kind of
work. She loves being able to paint her
favourite characters from that time and
dreaming up new ones of her own – especially
characters who can fly, because that is
something she has always wished to do herself.

The degree of finish in Julie Bell's paintings
works on what she calls the Papa Bear, Mama
Bear, Baby Bear principle. That is, elements
get finished according to their degree of

104 Hard Curves

Title: Colossus, 1993
Medium: Oil and Acrylic
Size: 11 x 15 in (28 x 38 cm)
Trading Card, Marvel Comics

One of the artist's first three Marvel trading cards, along with Iron Man and Silver Surfer. Their reception was one of Julie's magic moments in life as no-one, even herself, had seemed to have much confidence in her ability to deliver the goods. 'But they had to pick themselves up off the floor before saying how much they loved them.'

Title: Silver Surfer, 1993
Medium: Oil and Acrylic
Size: 11 x 15 in (28 x 38 cm)
Trading Card, Marvel Comics

Why Marvel are so delighted with Julie's first picture for them should be plain from this character, which perfectly combines her love of painting metal and the human form.

Title: Iron Man 1993
Medium: Oil on Acrylic
Size: 11 x 15 in (28 x 38cm)
Trading Card, Marvel Comics

importance in the picture. Backgrounds are secondary, but for that very reason they can often be great fun. There is the pleasure of creation without the graft of carrying the idea through to completion.

Generally the artist tries not to plan too much ahead. She decides mentally on the conditions of the setting, temperature, humidity, lighting and so on, then just starts painting and makes things up as she goes along. The process consists as much in taking paint off the surface with turps as in brushing it on, and feels much like sculpture.

Swamps and jungles are great fun, but so too are futuristic cityscapes. As a child, Julie was always drawn to architectural paintings, and loved to imagine what was behind this or that doorway or around the

Title: Dane, 1993
Medium: Oil and Acrylic
Size: 11 x 15 in (28 x 38 cm)
Cover, Image Comics

Dane™ and © Aegis
Entertainment, Inc. dba
Wildstorm Productions, 1995.
All rights reserved.

One of the things Julie enjoys
about her involvement in comics
is that it is a very masculine
environment and she enjoys
being one of the buddies. She
also enjoys handling characters
like Dane here in as macho a
way as any male artist.

The artist really enjoyed painting
this ice and, as it was winter at the
time, was not short of reference
material. In addition she collected
some crystal statues to get the feel
of working with transparency.
The fire in the background creates
an interesting contrast and
makes the figure look almost
as if it is melting.

corners of the buildings. Much the same holds with her own
creations, but with the added pleasure that in futuristic scenes there
are no rules or limits to the possible.

A large part of this comes from the circumstances in which Julie
Bell grew up, because her father is an architect and she used to love
the paintings he did of his projects. He wanted to be an artist himself
once, but the ambition has had to take a back seat to his profession
for the past forty years or so.

So what does he think of Julie's paintings? 'He's happy that I'm
doing something with art, I think; and he likes some of what I've

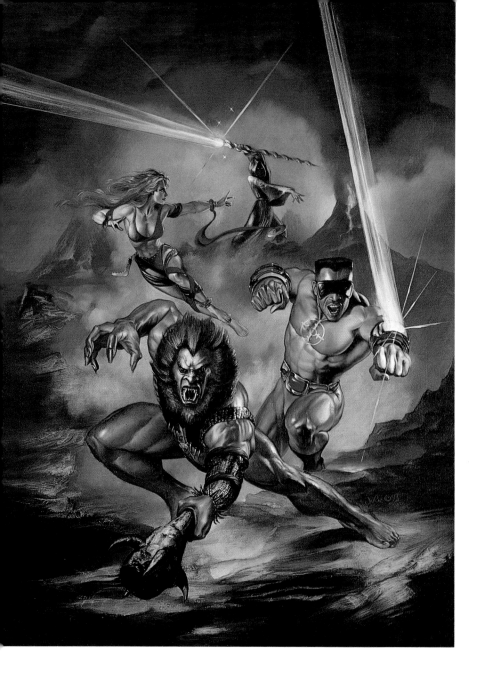

Title: Invincible Team, 1993
Medium: Oil and Acrylic
Size: 15 x 20 in (38 x 51 cm)
Video Game Cover: Sega Genesis

In general the artist prefers a single focus
in a picture, but she is aware that some
people prefer pictures like this where the
eye can wander around a bit, so she quite
enjoys the challenge. It illustrated a game
called *Eternal Champions* and she is very
happy with the way it turned out.

done, but he doesn't really understand or relate to fantasy. He
says things like, "Is there really a market for this kind of work?
Wouldn't you like to do something like Norman Rockwell?"'

The artist laughs a throaty Texan chuckle when relating this
comment of her father's. Julie laughs easily in conversation and
comes across as being very much at peace with both the world
and her private life. Fantasy is not an area of art in which she
ever seriously expected to find her niche; but having found a
space in which to exercise her imagination, she is determinedly,
cheerfully and very skilfully pushing back the boundaries at an
astonishing rate.

Title: Champions of the City, 1993 ▷
Medium: Oil and Acrylic
Size: 15 x 20 in (38 x 51 cm)
Video Game Cover,
Super Nintendo

The characters for this game, *Double Dragon II*, were already established but it still felt creative bringing them to life like this.

◁ *Title:* The Strangers, 1994
Medium: Oil and Acrylic
Size: 15 x 20 in (38 x 51 cm)
Cover, Malibu Comics

Title: Sabre-Toothed Snake, 1992 ▷
Medium: Oil and Acrylic
Size: 15 x 20 in (38 x 51 cm)
Video Game Cover: Super Nintendo

Although there are three main figures in this painting, they are dominated by the snake, which pulls the whole thing together. In the game it is only one of many perils faced by the adventurers.

Superheroes 109

5

Bodybuilding

A lot of people, especially women, are taught to be humble and demure, not to call attention to themselves. But people like to see others having a good time expressing themselves, whether it's in bodybuilding, painting or anything else. Even if someone's doing a terrible job, it's still good to watch if they're enjoying themselves. If something is part of you, you should try and capitalize on it.

Bodybuilding is at the heart of Julie Bell's art. 'These paintings are basically all about bodies,' she explains. 'Fantasy and superhero paintings are figure studies and I like the fact that they need to be superbly muscled, it makes for a more dynamic picture.' The first time she saw a female bodybuilder, though, she was quite bothered by the muscularity because it was so different from the way women usually look: 'I thought, what the heck is this? It's hard to see the beauty till you learn to understand and trust what is going on.

Photograph by John Nafpliotis

The artist in her days as a competitive bodybuilder, *c.* 1989.

'So the attraction to bodybuilding at first was not that I wanted to look like them but that I wanted to bring something out of myself.' Once involved, however, she came to feel that the common idea of how women's bodies should be needs changing.

She was involved in competitive bodybuilding for five years, and has trophies and titles to show for it. It gave her an understanding of how the human form works and how muscles interact during motion, which has proved invaluable in painting: 'It's especially useful portraying big men because not every muscle gets enlarged with training. You have to get the proportions right – you can tell when artists don't really understand. Also there are things that make the body express itself differently, like the size of the waist. The smaller it is, the more graceful the figure; a larger waist suggests strength. A lot of times you're playing with that grace/power compromise.

Julie Bell in 1995,
photographed by
Boris Vallejo.

Title: War Hero, 1993 ▷
Medium: Oil and Acrylic
Size: 15 x 20 in (38 x 51 cm)
Video Game Cover,
Goodtimes Home Video

The model for this hero is a butcher
in the artist's local grocery store.
Obviously not someone to quibble
with about short measures. He is also a
bodybuilder and appears in other
paintings, including the one opposite.

◁ *Title:* Tainted Claws, 1991
Medium: Oil on Acrylic
Size: 15 x 20 in (38 x 51 cm)
Portfolio Piece

A sample aimed at securing a commission
for *Conan* book covers. Successfully, as it
turned out, the two resulting covers being
shown later in this chapter. The title is an
essential ingredient of the picture, as without
it one could be forgiven for thinking Conan
was giving the poor creature a hard time.

Title: Judgement Day, 1994 ▷
Medium: Oil and Acrylic
Size: 15 x 20 in (38 x 51 cm)
Unpublished

Commissioned for a computer
game called *Doom II*, this image
was not used in the end, which
was disappointing as it had gone
backwards and forwards to the
publishers a few times to get it
right. Whatever the reason for it
not being used, it was probably
not that the creature looks
too much of a wimp.

Title: Demon in the Palace, 1992
Medium: Oil and Acrylic
Size: 15 x 20 in (38 x 51 cm)
Video Game Cover:
Sega Genesis

Boris was the model for the
demon, and Moorish reference
material was used to lend
authenticity to the background.

'Also I learned a lot about life through bodybuilding. The same
lessons could be applied to painting later. I learned how to push
myself way beyond what I thought I was capable of doing. John
Parrillo, who helps a lot of bodybuilders, once forced me to keep
on doing leg exercises till I collapsed. I'd never do it again but it
taught me a lot.'

Julie also enjoyed the performance aspect: 'I love attention, and
showing what I've worked hard to do. A lot of people, especially
women, are taught to be humble. But if something is part of you
I don't believe it should be suppressed. I first realized I loved the
spotlight when I did ballet – that feeling of "I've won! I love
this!". I'm not on stage in the same way with art but there's the
same feeling of showing the world what I've done, and I love it.'

Title: Haunted House, 1992
Medium: Oil and Acrylic
Size: 15 x 20 in (38 x 51 cm)
Video Game Cover: Sega Genesis

At first Julie really did not like this picture, particularly the monster, which she found horribly ugly. Over time, though, she has really grown to love it and it now reminds her of *Bugs Bunny*. She believes she may just have taken it too seriously at the time, plus there was the insecurity of it being a totally invented creature.

Title: Night of the Killer Mechs, 1992
Medium: Oil and Acrylic
Size: 15 x 20 in (38 x 51 cm)
Video Game Cover, Sega Genesis

For a change, the artist enjoys inventing machines like this, but never more than figure painting and she suspects her interest would soon flag if too much of it came her way.

Title: Cave of Darkness, 1992
Medium: Oil and Acrylic
Size: 15 x 20 in (38 x 51 cm)
Book Cover, Tor Books

To her knowledge, Julie Bell was the first female artist to illustrate *Conan* and one result is that the females in this pair of paintings are active participants in the action, rather than victims or slaves. The model for Conan was Darryl James, a bodybuilder whose muscles have barely been exaggerated, and whose fine sense of drama makes him a perfect model.

Title: Samurai, 1994
Medium: Oil and Acrylic
Size: 15 x 20 in (38 x 51 cm)
Publicity, Sega Genesis

This was intended for use as a large cardboard cutout display figure in stores to promote a video game, but the plan fell through. At some point a background will be added so this is probably the only time it will be printed in this form.

Julie took up bodybuilding in 1983, encouraged by her former husband, for which she remains grateful. She was prompted to take it up when she noticed how her arm muscles had developed through carrying the kids and chopping wood at home. She began fooling around with some weights of her husband's, and rediscovered the pleasure of that kind of physical activity. Even at elementary school she had been

Title: Dangerous Journey, 1992
Medium: Oil and Acrylic
Size: 15 x 20 in (38 x 51 cm)
Book Cover, Tor Books

As the stories for these two Conan
paintings had not yet been written, the
artist's brief was a fairly loose one.
Almost the only advice she was given
was, 'What sells these books is a good
butt on the cover.' Which she was happy
to oblige with, on the principle that
'Women can have a good butt and still
be in control of their lives.' The female
model here was a Shakespearian actress.

Title: Battle Cry, 1992
Medium: Oil and Acrylic
Size: 15 x 20 in (38 x 51 cm)
Video Game Cover, Sega Genesis

Julie likes horses a lot, at least she likes painting them. Her sister once kept two more or less wild ones. They could be ridden but had not been trained and once one of them kicked the artist in the face. She was lucky to escape with no more than a broken jaw and has since preferred to admire them from a safe distance.

Title: Savage Land, 1991
Medium: Oil and Acrylic
Size: 15 x 20 in (38 x 51 cm)
Video Game Cover, Sega Genesis

All pictures are a learning experience to an extent, says the artist, but some more than others, as in this case. This was her first video game illustration and she was very unsure how to handle it. For the skeleton she strung up a plastic model like a puppet and played with it till it seemed to fit the action. In retrospect she thinks the painting has a 'really fun, cartoon feel'.

Title: Battle of Stonehenge, 1991
Medium: Oil and Acrylic
Size: 15 x 20 in (38 x 51 cm)
Book Cover, Tor Books

For a novel by Harry Harrison being republished under a new cover. It was a novelty to be able to read the story before illustrating it.

interested: she once won a prize for doing more chin-ups than anyone else, and she loved competitive sports – but not team events. Bodybuilding also appealed because not many women did it. It became a key part of her life, and her days still begin with a session at the gym.

Going to the gym led to competitive bodybuilding. But she reached a point where the only way forward was to use steroids: 'The point of

Title: Wrestlers, 1993
Medium: Oil and Acrylic
Size: 15 x 20 in (38 x 51 cm)
Video Game Cover,
Super Nintendo

Two characters from the artist's gym.
Some who go there are professional
models anyway and only a few of those
approached have ever turned down the
chance to appear in a painting.

Julie©93

Title: Darryl & the Iguana, 1993
Medium: Oil and Acrylic
Size: 15 x 20 in (38 x 51 cm)
Portfolio Piece

An early figure study, later
completed as a fantasy picture.

Based on a photograph of the artist
and Boris Vallejo taken around the
time of their marriage.

Title: To Fly Again, 1993
Medium: Pencil
Size: 11 x 15 in (28 x 38 cm)
Portfolio Piece

From a photograph of the artist by
Boris Vallejo. There are plans for the
design to be made into jewellery
as part of a whole range of such
work based on bodybuilding.

Title: Metal Fantasy, 1994
Medium: Oil and Acrylic
Size: 15 x 20 in (38 x 51 cm)
Portfolio Piece

The contrast here is between the big,
powerful woman full of tenderness and
the small, shifty creature that looks
liable to bite off her nose. In the end
the creature seems to have more power.

Julie ©91

Title: Battle of the Mer, 1991
Medium: Oil and Acrylic
Size: 15 x 20 in (38 x 51 cm)
Portfolio Piece

The artist has yet to meet a woman who would not like to try the life of a mermaid. The fairytale of the *Little Mermaid* was one of her own favourites as a child. She knows there are questionable aspects of the story, but what counted most as a child was that it was about mermaids. Until about the time of this painting she knew little about the dark side of mermaids, their siren aspect, and was fascinated to read about it. So here, for dramatic contrast, we have one good and one bad mermaid fighting for the poor man in the foreground.

Title: Goldfish, 1993
Medium: Oil and Acrylic
Size: 11 x 15 in (28 x 38 cm)
Portfolio Piece

No drama here, just a beautiful mermaid suggested in part by the artist never having seen an Afro mermaid painting before. The model is again Linda Murray, who has inspired many of Julie Bell's favourite pictures.

bodybuilding is to develop yourself and push against the limits, but you have to keep a sense of proportion. I was never tempted by steroids, having known a lot of people who ruined their lives with drugs, and the lives of the people around them.'

Around this time Julie met Boris Vallejo. She was considering becoming a physical therapist or personal trainer, or becoming a medical illustrator, for which she was studying. But seeing his work opened a third door. It was one of those happy moments when disparate strands of life fuse together into a common purpose and nothing is quite the same again. Fantasy art beckoned and, buoyed by Boris' confidence that she had the talent, Julie took up the challenge.